Could Someone Wake Me Up Before I Drool on the Desk?

Books by Kevin Johnson

Early Teen Devotionals

Can I Be a Christian Without Being Weird?

Could Someone Wake Me Up Before I Drool on the Desk?

Does Anybody Know What Planet My Parents Are From?

Look Who's Toast Now!

So Who Says I Have to Act My Age?

Who Should I Listen To?

Why Can't My Life Be a Summer Vacation?

Why Is God Looking for Friends?

Books for Teens

Catch the Wave!

To find out more about Kevin Johnson's books,

visit his Web site: http://www.thewave.org

Could Someone Wake Me Up Before I

Before I

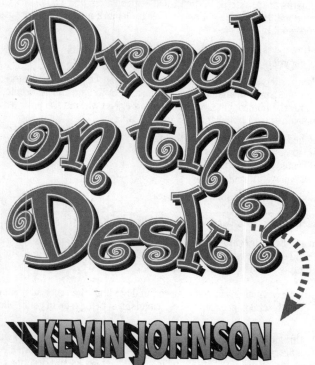

Drool on the Desk?

KEVIN JOHNSON

BETHANY HOUSE PUBLISHERS
MINNEAPOLIS, MN 55438

Published by Bethany House Publishers
A Ministry of Bethany Fellowship, Inc.
11300 Hampshire Avenue South
Minneapolis, Minnesota 55438

Printed in the United States of America.

Library of Congress Cataloging-in-Publication Data

Johnson, Kevin (Kevin Walter)
    Could someone wake me up before I drool on the desk? : conquering school and finding friends who count / Kevin W. Johnson.
        p. cm.
    Summary: Includes forty-five devotional readings that offer advice on dealing with school, peer pressures, friendships, being true to your beliefs, and more.

    1. Junior high school students—Prayer-books and devotions—English.
2. Teenagers—Prayer-books and devotions—English. 3. Christian life—Juvenile literature. [1. Christian life. 2. Prayer books and devotions.]
I. Title.
BV4850.J642   1995
242'.63—dc20   95-21321
ISBN 1-55661-416-0   CIP
                                                                                              AC

To my dad, Roy Johnson,
lifelong inner-city school teacher

and to teachers everywhere who
work hard not to put students to sleep.

KEVIN JOHNSON pastored a group of more than 400 sixth–ninth graders at Elmbrook Church in metro Milwaukee. While his training includes an M.Div. from Fuller Theological Seminary and a B.A. in English and Print Journalism from the University of Wisconsin-River Falls, his current interests run along the lines of cycling, guitar and shortwave radio. His eight-to-five pastime—editing books—takes place at Bethany House Publishers, where he is the senior editor for adult nonfiction. Kevin and his wife, Lyn, live in Minnesota with their two children, Nathaniel and Karin.

Contents

part 1

standin'
strong

1

If Jesus Showed Up at Your School

You'd seen Jesus at church before, but you'd never really been anywhere with Him. So you decided to invite Him to school for a day—sort of an experiment.

People warned you that Jesus would act odd and humiliate you in front of your school friends. They claimed they had thought about taking Him to school, too. But none of them had actually tried it.

Still, you were relieved that Jesus didn't look weird when He met you at the bus stop—none of that dusty ancient robe stuff. He looked clued in. He dressed normal. Pretty cool.

After English class Jesus said you were right—yes, Mr. Heffermeister truly was among the driest teachers in the entire universe—but that He had suffered through Mr. Heffermeister's lectures way longer than you had. Later in the day when Jesus fidgeted to get comfortable in a dwarfish desk, His knee welded with a wad of gum. *Good one, guys*, you thought. *What a way to impress Him with our school.*

You told Him that He could get the gum out with peanut butter. "But what about the grease blop," Jesus quizzed, "left by the peanut butter?" He said it was kind of like trying to fix problems without His help—our solutions only create more problems.

Deep. You wrote it all down to share in Sunday school. He said you should call it the "Parable of the Peanut Butter."

A couple of times classmates noticed Jesus squished in the desk next to you. You couldn't tell if they wanted to meet Him, so you joked and changed the subject. Jesus looked hurt. And one time you darted off, leaving Jesus dangling. You ran back. He was right where you left Him, waiting patiently. You promised not to do that again.

By the end of the day you and Jesus were chums. You asked Him to come to school again tomorrow to follow you around.

Jesus leaned over and whispered in your ear.

"Huh?" You're bewildered. "You want *me* to follow *you*?"

You may like school. You may hate it. You may endure it merely because you have to. Maybe you've jumped into middle school and think it's a blast—or maybe you're still feeling unsettled. And you might even be set to leap again into a new school.

You'll spend more than a million minutes in class before you graduate from high school. Not counting homework. Cheery thought.

Time doesn't fly when you're not having fun.

If you do like school there's a good chance it isn't because you actually like school. It's your friends. It's the fun you find on your own. But what if Jesus wants to come to *your* school? Won't that ruin everything?

Wrecking your life isn't part of His plan.

This book will help you see God's way to conquer school, get along with peers, and find friends who count. And it will show you one more crucial thing— how to run to God when everyone else lets you down.

The best way to use this book is to read one chapter a day. Don't forget to look up the Bible verses where it says ☑ **Read**. (That's really the most important part.) And if you want to dig even deeper, look up and read the Bible verses that pop up here and there in parentheses. Find a quiet place and make sure you have a Bible you can understand. (By the way, when you get to the last section of this book, don't pronounce the "P" in "Psalms," which is where those Bible readings come from. That would psound pstupid.)

Most importantly, ask Jesus to meet with you each time you read. He doesn't just want to be your friend at school. He wants to be with you right now.

2

Great Expectations

The night before Drew's first day of middle school he tossed frantically in his sleep. "NO! NOT THERE!" he screamed as his elementary school teachers dragged him toward the gaping mouth of a raging monster. And there at the monster's mouth stood Drew's parents, propping open the front doors of his new school. Drew's mom had that sorry look she got when he was little and he had to drop his drawers at the doctor's for a shot. His dad yelled as Drew's teachers tossed him in: "This hurts us more than it hurts you!"

The doors snapped shut behind Drew. Like a gargantuan tongue, the crowds inside swished him this way and that, and by the end of the day he felt as if he had been chewed to bits between overgrown molars.

He couldn't wait for the final bell to signal the school to spit him out.

📝 **Read Joshua 1:1–11. What does God promise to do for you when you go to school?**

God was prodding His people, the Israelites, to enter the incredible land He had promised to them. They knew all along that Moses, their leader, wouldn't go with them. But the people feared that with Moses gone their lives would never be the same. Not that they always liked Moses. Things just seemed normal—safe—when he was around.

The Israelites had nothing to fear. God, in fact, had promised success, provided they stuck close to Him. It didn't matter that they had no idea where they were going. They knew their Lord. They knew His Law—the commandments He had given them. Three times God reminded Joshua and the people: "Be strong! Be strong! BE STRONG!"

When you move to middle school, you leave elementary school behind. And it's gone—except for a head busting with facts and a few fun memories of recess. What made your life "normal" is dead.

Yet God says you have nothing to fear. He doesn't toss you all alone to the next stage in life. He swears to stay by your side and teach you *His* way to do school. And He'll show you how to conquer the monster.

Have I not commanded you? Be strong and courageous. Do not be terrified; do not be discouraged, for the LORD your God will be with you wherever you go.

JOSHUA 1:9

3

She's Nothing Like Her Sister

Megan cringed when Mrs. Grozny's eyebrow arched. She recognized that look. "Megan?" her teacher had said cheerily as she called roll on the first day of class. Then Mrs. Grozny spotted Megan. When she got a good look at Megan she glanced down quickly at her class list. "Megan *Ronson*?" And the raised eyebrow said it all: *You look like Tina. You'd better not act like her.*

"She knows your sister, Megan," someone across the aisle teased. "She thinks you're Tina."

There wasn't a kid in school who hadn't heard of Megan's older sister. No one would ever forget that three years ago Tina was expelled for selling drugs and then tried to torch the school. "She thinks you're Tina the Terrorist!"

I'm not my sister! Megan wanted to say. *Give me a chance!*

▶ **Read Psalm 139:1–6. Who knows the real you—and who you can be?**

They don't see you. They see what they *think* you are. You remind them of an older brother who was so bad that you never get a chance to be good. Or they remember your sister who was so smart and sickly sweet that you can't compete. Even people who don't compare you to brothers or sisters want to label you and stuff you in a box. They remember every time you've embarrassed yourself from third grade on—they won't let you escape. They never forget your flubs—they don't let you change.

They want to define you. Design you. If you let them tell you who you are and who you can be, you're trapped. Boxed in.

But they don't understand you like God does. He's searched you and knows you—your every thought, word, and action. He saw you before you were born (Psalm 139:15–16). And He wants you to live without comparing yourself—or letting yourself be compared—to other people (Galatians 6:4).

You don't figure out who you are by listening to people who pin you in, but by seeing yourself through the eyes of the One who knows you best. God blows the tops off their boxes. He sets you loose to follow Him and become what He made you to be.

O LORD, you have searched me and you know me.

PSALM 139:1

4

Crawling the Walls

"Class, I'm going to step down to the office for twenty minutes," your teacher tells you and your cohorts. "I want you to remain at your desks, studying pages 643 to 678 of your social studies textbook."

Party! everyone thinks. *She didn't just say she was leaving. She said where she was going. And how long!* As your teacher toddles down the hall, the lookouts scramble. *She's gone!* Chips and two-liter bottles of soda appear from nowhere. Guys break out cards. Girls disco on desks.

You, however, dutifully read your assignment as paper airplanes and footballs fly overhead. You pass page 678 and zoom toward page 700—thanks to the lessons on study skills your youth pastor taught—until the rest of the class notices you.

They pelt you with garbage.

Read Colossians 3:22–24. You know you're not supposed to crawl the walls at school. But why not?

Your class probably wouldn't riot if your teacher left the room. Then again, maybe it would. But if it did, you probably wouldn't be the only one not goofing off. Then again, maybe you would. Or maybe—just maybe—you would lead the revolt.

The choice you make all starts with one question: Does school rot or not?

The slaves Paul wrote to seldom suffered as badly as slaves in America. More than half the people in major Roman cities were slaves, including most teachers and doctors. Still, the slaves were property controlled by owners. They did what they were told.

They couldn't do much about their bondage. But they could alter their attitude.

Like you at school. If school is something you just endure, you'll have to grab your desk until your knuckles go pale to make yourself be good. Paul told the slaves, though, that there was a way to *want* to do what they had to do anyway: When they did their work, they could make up their minds that they were working for God.

You don't do school for the teacher who puts you to sleep. God is the reason you struggle through your homework, listen in class, stay clear of trouble. Doing school God's way starts with doing school for Him.

Slaves, obey your earthly masters in everything; and do it, not only when their eye is on you and to win their favor, but with sincerity of heart and reverence for the Lord.

COLOSSIANS 3:22

Catch this: Paul, by the way, isn't defending slavery. He's recognizing it as reality. In 1 Corinthians 7:21–24 Paul taught that slaves should get free when they could. He wrote in Galatians 3:28 that Christian slaves and masters were complete equals—a statement that prodded American Christians to work to abolish the evil of slavery.

5

Blowin' in the Wind

They had a deal. Dirk, Ben, and Chester ate together. Every day. Then none of them would look stupid eating all by his lonesome.

At the opposite end of the lunchroom from where they usually sat was a table that oozed cool—occupied by girls who make guys gawk and guys who cause girls to flock.

One day when Dirk approached the cool table, its occupants stared him down. They might forgive him this once if he crawled quickly back where he belonged. Then they saw who he was with. One of their own. They let Dirk in—for today, anyway.

Ben and Chester stood up to watch Dirk and Theresa find seats. As Dirk eased into coolness they almost applauded. They waited for his signal inviting them over. But when Dirk sat down to eat they figured it out.

They'd been forgotten. They'd been ditched.

Dirk. What a jerk.

Read Romans 15:5–7. How do friends stay friends—and make more friends?

When you're friendless you blow through school like tumbleweed. You're barely part of the landscape.

You don't think you matter much. You feel dried up and ugly, and occasionally you get burned to keep other people warm.

With friends, you don't feel alone. You feel okay. Valuable. You belong.

Making great friends is a great thing. Except when it kills other friendships.

Paul hints in the chapter before the passage you read that you make friends and stay friends (you have a "spirit of unity") when you work hard to pull people together instead of pushing them apart—especially if you pull together around Christ.

Paul says your goal is no less than to accept other people the way God accepts you—welcoming them into your group, onto your turf, treating them the way you want to be treated (Matthew 7:12). You might fool yourself into thinking that the way to the top is to dump your musty old friends and chum with the cool ones. But God's at the top. And He wants everyone in His circle of friends (2 Peter 3:9). He never forms a ring with His friends that's so tight there isn't room for more.

———————

Accept one another, then, just as Christ accepted you,
in order to bring praise to God.

Romans 15:7

6

Top Dog

Shawna glanced at her grade, cracked a twisted smile, and looked around to see what everyone else got on the test. Her classmates hid their papers. They knew she did better. She always did better.

So Shawna snatched Eric's test. He was so nice—but so slow at school. "Give it back!" Eric begged, looking like he was going to bawl.

Shawna sneered. "Maybe you should sit in the back with the drugheads," she advised. "They could tutor you. Maybe you'd pass."

You don't have to look hard to see plenty of people better than you at a lot of things. Even so, it's usually not tough to find people *worse* than you—or to notice that when they look bad you look good.

📝 **Read Galatians 6:3–5. How do you know when you've done well at something?**

If you bust the curve, you might think you did your best on a test. If your brother catches the blame for everything bad, you might be content with how you act at home. Or if you know less about the Bible than your Christian friends, you might conclude you're a slug.

When you take a test, the curve counts. But

grades don't tell the whole story—like whether anything lodged in your brain long-term. Dodging your parents' wrath might merely mean that you're good at hiding what you do behind their backs. Feeling less "spiritual" than your friends doesn't show whether you're getting to know God better.

If how you seem to stack up against others determines what you think or feel about yourself, then you're using a yardstick that's never the same length twice. And you'll either squish people with your huge head or feel tiny and worthless.

When you measure yourself against God's standard of how to think and act—the yardsticks you find in the Bible—you see that all of us fall short of God's perfection (Romans 3:23). Yet you also see what you're shooting for. And the same God who shows you the real you—the good, bad, and ugly—promises to remake you (Romans 14:4).

Then you can pat yourself on the back without putting other people down.

Each one should test his own actions. Then he can take pride in himself, without comparing himself to somebody else. . . .

GALATIANS 6:4

7

Waiting for the Candy to Drop

I've read this sixteen times. With her head in her hands, Kendra peeked through her fingers at her math book. *I still don't get it.*

Math is so stupid, she decided as she knocked her book onto the floor. She felt bad when a bunch of pages got bent. What worried her, though, was that *she* might be what was stupid. Seeing a math aide three days a week had helped Kendra keep up—until this year. She *wanted* to work hard and do well! Other subjects were tough, but nothing like math. Every study session was like starting over, as if each night someone stuck a syringe in her skull and sucked out her brains while she slept.

She mulled over her choices: Pretend school doesn't matter. Buy a bunch of makeup and hope she makes it as a model. Plan on bagging groceries for the rest of her life.

God, Kendra prayed, *you said you would be with me wherever I went. So where are you? Why is this so hard?*

▶ **Read Isaiah 41:8–16. If God is with you, why doesn't He fix your problems right away?**

Worms. They spend life digging dirt. Then they get smooshed on the sidewalk. Or bit in half by a bird. Or stuck with a fishhook. Or they just disappear into the ground.

You're not a worm. God made you glorious (Psalm 8:3–9). But that doesn't mean you never feel a little slimy.

God is with you when things go well. He's also there when things go awful and you feel wormish. He doesn't promise to stick with you only if you get all your math problems right—because you're a wonderful person. Not one of us is that wonderful. God stays with you because you belong to Him. You're "His servant," chosen for a privileged position. You're His handpicked friend, destined to thrash your mountainous obstacles.

It's tense, though, in the time gap between your problems and God's provisions, between your hurt and God's help. God isn't a candy machine you can rock until the good stuff drops. But know this for sure: He also isn't a candy machine that swallows your money and leaves you empty-handed. He takes care of what you give to Him.

Problems now. Provision in God's time. In the meantime? *Trust.*

So do not fear, for I am with you; do not be dismayed, for I am your God. I will strengthen and help you; I will uphold you with my righteous right hand.

ISAIAH 41:10

8

Nowhere to Go

Older guys surrounded Branston and his friends as they walked home from school. The biggest kid grabbed Branston. "I saw you sneaking around. You stay out of my face."

"Out of your face? I was just walking home. I wasn't anywhere near you." The thug hit Branston with a half-punch, half-slap, full wallop. Branston's head snapped to the side and his lip gushed blood.

Branston lived with both parents in a city flat in a tough neighborhood. They never made enough money to move away. When his parents bussed him to a school in the 'burbs, kids teased him. Once they tossed whopper firecrackers toward him to see him dive. A split second later he figured out it wasn't a gun—but he'd been made a fool.

He wanted a place where he fit. He wanted someplace safe. He didn't know where it was. He for sure didn't know how to get there.

> Read 2 Chronicles 14:11. What is "trusting God"?

Some problems—at school or home or with friends, or maybe with your health—get so big that you can't budge them. You feel like an old beater car stuck in a trash smasher. The walls are closing in. No escape routes. You know you're supposed to trust God—and you're supposed to know how. But how?

The verse you read picks up in the middle of a description of how King Asa of Judah and his troops squared off against a vast army of Cushites. Asa's actions show what to do when there's not much you *can* do: He prayed. Then he obeyed. That's trust.

Asa reminded God—and himself—that there was no one as powerful as God, and that God alone was their hope. Then King Asa led the Israelite army into battle, confident that God was with them. God crushed the Cushites.

But the end of the story isn't so happy. Late in life Asa refused to depend on God and do what he knew was right. He bought help from an evil army and sought healing from occult doctors. Even when a prophet reminded Asa that ". . . the eyes of the LORD range throughout the earth to strengthen those whose hearts are fully committed to him" (2 Chronicles 16:9), Asa refused to trust in God—to pray and obey. His nation remained at war. His illness got worse.

Asa forgot. He had something better than *somewhere* to go. He had *Someone*.

Then Asa called to the LORD his God and said, "LORD, there is no one like you to help the powerless against the mighty. Help us, O LORD our God, for we rely on you, and in your name we have come against this vast army. O LORD, you are our God; do not let man prevail against you."

2 CHRONICLES 14:11

9

The Art of Endurance

Morning after morning you slam the alarm clock, crawl from bed, board a bus, trudge through the school, and take your seat in your first-hour art class.

Once you clocked your teacher saying *"Um"* forty-eight times in six minutes. At forty-eight you fell into a coma. After you regained consciousness, you killed time by plucking out your eyebrows hair by hair, but that only lasted a few days.

The way you see it, the system is taunting you. You feel you have no choice but to go deviant. While the class makes metal stick figures, you manufacture a miniature spring-loaded catapult to launch notes to a friend at another table. When the class builds a gargantuan log cabin out of tongue depressors to commemorate Abraham Lincoln's birthday, you hang sticks from your nose. And then one day you rewire the pottery wheel to pep it up. Your clay flies. It *thwonks* your teacher on the head. You get detention.

More excitement.

▶ **Read Galatians 6:7–10. How do you cope when school bores you silly?**

Some days at school you feel like you should have unscrewed your brain and left it at home—you didn't need it. Or a teacher doesn't care about what he's teaching—so neither do you. Or you can't see what school has to do with real life because you have more important things knotting your mind—like parents separating, friends with problems or problems with friends, or a dad or mom losing a job, or worse.

Peers try anything to bust the boredom, from talking when it's time to zip lips, to going to school high. What will *you* do?

Work can be boring—until you get paid. Doing good at school or anywhere else can be boring—until you see the reward.

God doesn't give gold stars for acting good. He gives gifts because *He's* good, not because you are (Titus 3:4–7). But doing what's right, keeping at it, allowing God to enter your life and remake you, is like putting seed in the ground. Sooner or later plants sprout. In time you reap peace and a satisfaction that God is right and you did right (Hebrews 12:11).

And that's no bore.

The one who sows to please his sinful nature, from that nature will reap destruction; the one who sows to please the Spirit, from the Spirit will reap eternal life. Let us not become weary in doing good, for at the proper time we will reap a harvest if we do not give up.

GALATIANS 6:8–9

10
Spit Out Ze Bones

The girls looked up to her. The guys just stared at her. So when the seventeen-year-old Olympic hopeful stepped up to speak at the school assembly, everyone hushed.

"When I sprint, I imagine myself flying through the air," she told them. "In my mind, my feet barely touch the ground. You have the same power inside you to unlock all that you can be. What's the key? Believe in yourself. If you believe hard enough you make things happen. You can change what you become.

"In your mind you can picture yourself beating the person running in the lane next to you. You can think your way to straight A's. You can make yourself a millionaire by picturing it in your mind. You can even stop your little sister from being a brat. Just imagine it and you have it."

✐ **Read Proverbs 3:5–8. What makes you sure of yourself?**

You're no doubt certain of your ability to simultaneously walk and chew gum. Or to pat your head and rub your tummy. Still, there are other times you're not so sure of yourself. You need a boost to help you keep from whiffing, biffing, fumbling, or crumbling.

Rehearsing the situation in your mind may help.

But it doesn't change reality. If you could imagine your way to the Olympics you'd be able to high jump fifty-three feet by now.

You can have great confidence—through God. Think about these verses: "With your help I can advance against a troop; with my God I can scale a wall" (Psalm 18:29). And "I can do everything through him who gives me strength" (Philippians 4:13). Even so, God gently reminds us of this: "Without me you can do nothing" (John 15:5 NKJV). Our brains aren't as big as we think. We're not as strong or wise as our eyes sometimes tell us.

No matter where you go to school you can't swallow whole what you hear and see: "Depend on yourself." "Just accept what I say. Trust me." "The Bible is full of myths." "Ignore your parents. Make your own decisions." Or "Leaders always know what's right." God gave you the Bible to help you separate truth from lies (2 Timothy 3:14–16).

When you eat fish, you eat the meat and leave the bones. You'll survive if you swallow a few tiny bones. But if you don't strain out the big ones you'll gag. Or choke and die.

Trust in the LORD *with all your heart and lean not on your own understanding. . . .*

PROVERBS 3:5

The Easiest Way to Get Through School

While Neil's classmates spent five weeks in the library pillaging dusty books and encyclopedias, he studied back issues of *Sports Illustrated* and *Mad*. He snickered when the class egghead inquired how his research on the feeding habits of Galapagos tortoises was coming along. He roared when kids carried home piles of books. "You don't have to do all that," he informed them. "The teacher's just trying to scare us."

This research paper, his teacher said, counted for half their quarter grade. There were no progress checks. They were trustworthy until they proved otherwise.

The night before the paper was due there was a good movie on TV, so Neil was glad his parents didn't know he had a whopper report to crank out. He ate popcorn and quaffed four cans of Mountain Dew. The next day everyone else turned in twenty-page laserfied reports with the required forty footnotes. Neil showed up with two pages scribbled in pencil off the top of his head.

A red *F* was the teacher's response.

📖 **Read Proverbs 4:3–13. What's the easiest way to get through school?**

You'll have nightmares about school for the rest of your life. You forget to go to class—all semester. You lose your locker combination. You misplace your schedule, and a lady in the office with an AK–47 makes you pay fifty bazillion dollars for a new one.

School can be scary. So how do you survive the nightmare right now?

Start by staying awake. Pay attention and take notes in class so you don't have to study so hard on your own. (You need to get a life if you have time to do something twice that you could have done only once.) Listen to teachers. Laugh back at peers who slam you for studying hard. Do your own work and remind yourself that most of the time hard work still pays off.

Getting smart doesn't mean becoming a wise guy, memorizing encyclopedias, dining on dictionaries, or kissing up to teachers.

It's knowing what your goal is and how to avoid the traps between you and your destination. It's figuring out the best way to get things done—following God's rules, staying within His boundaries of right and wrong and His guidelines of good, better, and best. That's what Proverbs calls wisdom.

It's easy. What you're supposed to do happens to be the smart thing to do.

Do not forsake wisdom, and she will protect you; love her, and she will watch over you. Wisdom is supreme; therefore get wisdom. Though it cost all you have, get understanding.

PROVERBS 4:6–7

12

Your Life in Pictures

You flip open your yearbook and spot your face spread on 22 of 36 pages. *You were magnificent.* You captained three teams, climbed your way to first-chair violin, and captured Student of the Year honors for your 4.0 grade-point average.

Or you've been bad—*really bad*—and you're splattered on just as many pages. Surprise! You were voted "Brat of the Year" and "Most likely to live in a home for juvenile delinquents."

Or you struggled along in the middle of the pack—and *no one knows you were there.* You didn't get voted "best dressed" or "best personality" or even "class brain." It takes three passes through the book to find a single tiny picture of you. Page 31, bottom inside corner, it's you with the flu. Even in black-and-white you look green.

☑ **Read 2 Corinthians 3:18. Three questions: Why do you go to school? What will you be remembered for? What will you accomplish?**

There are more efficient ways to do school if your sole reason for being there is to absorb facts. The custodians could hardwire you into a virtual reality system and give you a virtual brain. Or for a low-cost, low-tech education, teachers could lock you in solitary confinement with a textbook and give you something to eat only after you choked down algebra.

You need to learn school stuff so you don't spend your life refilling the burrito bar at Taco Tim's. And you pick up other skills at school too. Like how to get along with friends—and enemies. How to work with teachers—your bosses. How to keep going—when you'd rather quit.

God sends you to school for one more reason: to use the experience to remake you to look like Jesus, who knew God the Father totally (John 17:25–26), obeyed God willingly (John 6:38), and loved other people completely (John 15:13). People saw God's glory—God's greatness—reflected in Jesus, just like they can see it in you. Jesus didn't "veil" or hide God's glory shining in Him. He didn't wear a bag to hide who He was.

You may not rate a ton of pictures in the yearbook. Your classmates may not recall what you did. But hopefully they'll still remember *who* you looked like.

———————

And we, who with unveiled faces all reflect the Lord's glory, are being transformed into his likeness with ever-increasing glory, which comes from the Lord, who is the Spirit.

2 CORINTHIANS 3:18

part 2

gettin'
along

13

Think Small to Think Big

Alisha elbows Bill. "Isn't that the boy who moved in across the street from you?" The guy she points out mopes down the hallway at school all alone. He doesn't look at anyone—he looks afraid. He stops to stare out a window.

"I guess so," Bill answers. "He was at the bus stop this morning. He sat a couple seats away from me in—would you quit looking over there? He'll see us." He turns the other way so the new kid doesn't spot him.

Alisha glares at Bill. "You're pathetic. I'm going to go say hi and welcome him to school."

"Just leave him alone," Bill argues. "I'm sure he'll make friends. He's fine. He has to fend for himself like everyone else."

Bill pulls at Alisha when she starts to head in the new kid's direction. "Let's *go*," Bill begs. "He'll think I want to be his best friend or something."

☑ **Read Mark 9:33–37. Jesus has been walking down a road with His disciples. What does it mean to be "like Christ"?**

What would you say if someone asked you why you're here on planet earth? Are you here just to consume oxygen? To master video games? To inhale the contents of your parents' refrigerator—excluding the vegetable drawer? To rule the world?

Think bigger.

You're here to live like Christ. You're destined to do the things He did (Ephesians 2:10). You're here, in short, to be a servant like your Master. But what does *that* look like?

Jesus had just told His disciples that He would suffer and die. They didn't get it. They thought that to be Jesus—God's Son—was to rule the world and crush the opposition. They thought that to be His follower was to rule with Him and squish people they detested. They didn't understand that being like Him meant serving like Him.

Jesus-style servanthood isn't made up of acts like helping old ladies across the street. It's a way of life, caring even for "insignificant" people—like little kids. And your enemies. And "losers." People you know and people you don't. It's learning to show love to everyone around you.

Sitting down, Jesus called the Twelve and said, "If anyone wants to be first, he must be the very last, and the servant of all."

MARK 9:35

14
Redo Your Attitude

Michelle rolled over, glanced at the clock, groaned, and bolted. *Not again!* She had eight minutes to master a disaster. Nothing clean to wear—everything was in the washer, sopping wet. She pulled her clumpy, wangy sleep hair into a ponytail and tugged on a baseball cap, even though she knew her teachers wouldn't let her keep it on.

A sprint to the bus stop saved her a long, late walk to school, and she dropped panting into the first open seat. Bad choice. Kaytlin smiled sweetly at Michelle. "Sleep through your alarm again, Shelly?" she inquired. "That's twice this week, isn't it?"

Kaytlin had once loaned a stack of teen magazines to Michelle. Feeling like Kaytlin's woefully average neighbor, Michelle toiled to follow their beauty tips. It was like trying to follow a blueprint for a bomber. So today Michelle spent the ride to school wishing Kaytlin would get the chicken pox, the mumps, and fat all at the same time. And she dreamed what it would be like to have Kaytlin's flawless face and bikini body.

Michelle wanted plastic surgery on her life.

▶ **Read Titus 3:3–8. How do you put a stop to jealousy?**

Jealousy doesn't end when you get what someone else has, because you'll always find someone else who still has more. Even the beautiful and bulked-up people feel left out. Miss Americas claw and whine to get their own talk shows, and Superbowl winners turn into armchair-quarterbacking couch potatoes. And they hate people who have what they want, whether it's more looks, muscles, money, or popularity.

The only hope is to be happy with what *you* have. God doesn't do plastic surgery to make you into someone else. He does a heart transplant to redo your attitude.

Paul told Titus that before we know God, we're wrapped up in malice (a desire to harm or spite others) and envy (unhappiness at what someone else has or can do). Yet when we accept God's kindness we begin to see we have everything we need most— God's acceptance, His forgiveness (we're "justified by His grace"), the promise of living in eternal paradise with God, and friendship right now with His Holy Spirit.

What others have that we don't is nothing compared to that.

At one time we too were foolish, disobedient, deceived and enslaved by all kinds of passions and pleasures. We lived in malice and envy, being hated and hating one another. But when the kindness and love of God our Savior appeared, he saved us. . . .

TITUS 3:3–5

15
Bragging Rights

"Strike three! That's the game!" the umpire hollered. Runners trotted in from first and third, and the scorekeeper recorded another loss for the Panthers. "You're out, son," the ump said a bit more gently as Troy stood stuck in the batter's box, still trying to figure out what had blown by him. "Next time."

Troy was barely out of the box when David pounced on him. "You whiffed! You always whiff! You lost the game!"

"Me? I wasn't the only one who got out," Troy shot back.

"But you're a loser. Almost the whole team is a bunch of losers. I don't know why I play on this team. I hit, I run, I score—then you whiff."

Jake joined David in walloping Troy, and others trotted over to see what the noise was about. "The two of us," Jake bragged, "could beat the rest of you put together."

➤ **Read Jeremiah 9:23–24. When is it okay to brag?**

You can argue with a friend about who's taller. But you both look short next to the starting center for the Lakers. You can debate who's smarter, but Einstein wouldn't have asked either of you for help with his homework. Likewise, God reminds us that next to Him we don't measure up. "To whom will you compare me?" God asks in Isaiah 40:25, "Or who is my equal?"

God's point isn't to pound us into the ground like a kid hunting ants with a baseball bat.

Here's His point: The things we trust in—and brag about—are by His standards imperfect, powerless, and broken down, like a batter in a slump. It's silly to feel overly proud of brains that leak, beauty that gets baggy, muscles that go flabby, and money that whooshes down the drain in ways we can't predict.

It's right to enjoy the good things God gives us. Even so, our confidence and security is God himself—not some nasty brute of a God, but One perfect in kindness and goodness. God is "righteous in all his ways and loving toward all he has made" (Psalm 145:17).

And having a friend like that *is* something worth bragging about.

This is what the LORD says: "Let not the wise man boast of his wisdom or the strong man boast of his strength or the rich man boast of his riches, but let him who boasts boast about this: that he understands and knows me, that I am the LORD, who exercises kindness, justice and righteousness on earth, for in these I delight," declares the LORD.

JEREMIAH 9:23–24

16

Don't Apologize for You

"That isn't the Little Dipper. It's *those*," Jamie argued. "Over *there*."

"Actually, it's that set of stars up there," Eileen said quietly. "See the handle? And the dipper?" Eileen was surprised. *They didn't laugh at me.* Dazzled by the night sky outside the city, kids on the church retreat actually seemed to listen to her. So Eileen pointed out some other constellations. Then Mars and Jupiter. One of the kids, though, said she was making stuff up. Eileen got quiet again.

"Ignore him," one of the adult leaders advised. Then he asked how she knew so much. Eileen never told anyone she was into astronomy. It would only make her feel even more like an alien. She didn't care about clothes, got bored putting on makeup, and thought boys making armpit noises needed to grow up. But this time she let some of her enthusiasm out. The leader thought Eileen should bring her telescope on the next retreat.

Maybe she would.

► **Read 1 Corinthians 12:14–21. Does being different mean you're weird?**

"Different" isn't high on your list of what you want to be when you grow up. You might like someone no one else likes, so you pretend to like someone popular who really makes you retch. Or you know that people are about to badmouth your music or your hobbies, so you strike—you laugh at them before they laugh at you, slam them before they slam you. True, sometimes it's socially acceptable to be strange—but only if the crowd says so.

Right before the passage you read, Paul explained that God gives every Christian a gift to use to strengthen other believers. (He lists some of the gifts in verses 8–10, others in Romans 12:4–8 and Ephesians 4:11–13.) Each gift is different. But each gift is necessary. And the worst thing that can happen is for someone to hide his or her gift.

People—at church, and in your school, family, and neighborhood—need you. God gave you gifts, tastes, experiences, and talents both natural and supernatural that you're to use to build others up. God didn't wire anyone weird—just unique.

And even if others don't know it, they can't live without you.

———————

Now the body is not made up of one part but of many. If the foot should say, "Because I am not a hand, I do not belong to the body," it would not for that reason cease to be part of the body.

1 CORINTHIANS 12:14–15

17
Just Kidding

He'll never talk to her, thinks Hugh. So he decides to help Mark out.

"Mark thinks you're beautiful," Hugh shouts at Danielle. She looks at Mark like he's a nerd on a stick. Mark clamps his hand over Hugh's mouth and drags him around the corner to slap him up. "Ha, ha, funny, funny," Mark says as he socks Hugh's stomach.

Later Hugh tapes a two-foot-high homemade Valentine on Danielle's locker, complete with a drooly poem and candy wax lips and Mark's name signed in big letters. Half the school reads it before Danielle gets to school and tears it down.

"Why did you do that?" Mark yells.

"It was funny," Hugh jokes. "You're so chicken."

Mark doesn't look amused. A few minutes and a lot of punches later, when both of them are wiping bloody noses on the way to the principal's office, Hugh still doesn't think it's a big deal.

What's wrong with him? wonders Hugh. *Can't he take a joke?*

☑ **Read Matthew 5:21–24. What do you do when you've made someone mad?**

The passage you read pictures a person busily worshiping God ("at the altar"), when he realizes he's angered someone. If that happens, Jesus said, the worshiper should go to the person he made mad and set things right.

Now picture this. You're sitting in church. You grow uneasy. A bit queasy. You break a sweat and dig for a motion-sickness bag in the pew rack. Suddenly you bolt screaming out the back to beg forgiveness from a person you hurt.

Highly unlikely.

When you blow it you might not even feel guilty, much less stabbed through the heart by the knowledge that you've done wrong. Jesus reminded His listeners that God hates not just "big sins" like murder, but "small sins" like anger. It's all the same in His eyes. And you don't want to wait to fix wrongs until they're so huge you can't help but feel miserable.

Your problem isn't solved by a secret "sorry" tossed at God. He wants you to go to the one you angered and repair what you can.

Even tough guys need to go and apologize. And set the situation straight. And change.

"Therefore, if you are offering your gift at the altar and there remember that your brother has something against you, leave your gift there in front of the altar. First go and be reconciled to your brother; then come and offer your gift."

MATTHEW 5:23–24

18
Don't Hire
a Hit Man

Sabina knew something was wrong as soon as she picked up her book bag. *This is too light,* she thought. She kicked herself for forgetting her homework—now, after tennis practice, everything at school but the phys ed area was locked up. But it took Sabina only a few seconds to recall she *had* put her homework in the bag.

Someone's been into my bag. Fumbling to unzip her bag, she dumped it upside down. Only two library books fell out—none of her spiral notebooks. Worst of all, her typed-up oral report and all the notes she used to put it together were gone.

The report was due tomorrow and her teacher had a "no excuses, no makeups" rule.

The next day Mr. Grady wouldn't buy Sabina's story about a stolen paper—even when a girl named Jessica stood up and read Sabina's report, word for word. With all her notes and everything gone, Sabina had no way to prove Jessica had read *her* paper.

It came Sabina's turn to report. She was dead.

☑ **Read Matthew 18:15–17. What do you do when someone treats you badly?**

Charging the front of the classroom probably won't wring a tearful confession from someone who wronged you. Neither will standing on a table in the lunchroom and screaming. Nor will whispering behind someone's back.

Jesus said the first step to take is usually the last one you want to. It's easier to moan to God. It's simpler to start a rumor. But it's also easier for a wrongdoer to admit he or she blew it when you talk one-on-one, in private. That's why Jesus said to talk *to*—not *about*—a person who hurts you.

(Some wrongs are so big and bad that it's smart to skip that first step. A victim of sexual abuse or some other crime, for example, shouldn't confront an attacker. She or he should run to parents, counselors, or police, whose job it is to help. The same is true if you witness something illegal.)

Getting help is what the next steps are all about. If the person you confront won't admit the wrong, take someone with you to strengthen what you say. And after that you can appeal to people in authority like parents, teachers, principals, or pastors.

You don't have to play dead when someone wrongs you. But you also don't have to hire a hit man.

"If your brother sins against you, go and show him his fault, just between the two of you. If he listens to you, you have won your brother over."

MATTHEW 18:15

50

19
Right Place, Right Time

Chad was waiting in line to buy movie tickets, joking with a clump of friends. When a group of guys from church walked up and spotted him, they looked less than jovial. Chad wasn't sure, but they seemed to be watching him.

Sitting in the movie, Chad couldn't figure out why his Christian friends were irate. He couldn't do everything with them. And he wasn't sneaking into some ghastly movie he shouldn't see. In fact, Chad knew his parents would never let him go to the movie he saw his Christian friends go into.

When Chad darted out to get a bucket of popcorn, one of his church friends followed him to the lobby. Jake pounced on him. "What are you doing with those guys?"

"They're my friends from down the block," Chad explained. "You know that."

Jake wasn't convinced. "You shouldn't hang around with them. They're going to ruin you. You're going to turn into one of them."

▶ **Read Luke 5:27–32. Should Christians have non-Christian friends?**

You'd know you were in the wrong place at the wrong time with the wrong crowd if cops busted down the doors of the house you were in and shot in tear gas.

People and places and situations don't have to be so unmistakably evil to be just as risky. The Bible, for example, makes clear that Christians shouldn't be "unequally yoked," roped together with non-Christians. Attachments like going together, dating, marriage—probably even being best friends—with people cold toward God sooner or later will keep you from obeying God (2 Corinthians 6:14).

But that doesn't mean you should run and hide from non-Christians. When the Pharisees criticized Jesus for spending time with sinners—including the lowest life form of that society, tax collectors—Jesus retorted that He was like an army medic rushing to help the wounded and dying.

He went where He was needed most. Jesus wasn't making an excuse to have the out-of-bounds fun He would miss if He stuck close to "nice" people. His goal was to invite people to meet God. What's yours?

Jesus answered them, "It is not the healthy who need a doctor, but the sick. I have not come to call the righteous, but sinners to repentance."

LUKE 5:31–32

20

O Playdough Day

Oh noooooo! Not again!

Splat. A fist slams you, shimmies and squooshes you this way and that, rolling you into a ball.

Oh noooooo! Not that!

It's intense tucked inside the Playdough press. Tiny holes dead ahead!

Oh noooooo! Not the stringy thingy!

You struggle uselessly as you're forced through itty bitty holes, shredded into a dozen strands—one big-time split personality, not to mention the splitting headache.

You're pinched and pressed and sliced with a plastic knife. You've been turned into hair and plastered onto a Playdough dog.

▶ **Read Galatians 1:3–12. Paul refuses to give into peer fear on one point in particular. What is it?**

You don't live in this world by yourself. It's crowded. You bump people. They shove you. They gang up and squish you. You inevitably get molded into a new shape.

So? You've heard that before. Parents, teachers, and tacky TV commercials have been telling you since you were two that peers can mislead and crush you.

But peer pressure isn't all bad. If it weren't for peer fear you'd still pick your nose in public. Deep down you know you can't live isolated from your peers, and a lot of times it's fine to want to fit in. Isn't a true nerd, after all, someone who lives in his or her own wee little world, clueless of when and how it's *okay* to conform?

Yet you can never be all your peers want you to be. Paul pointed out one area—your faith as a Christian—where it's never right to settle for being shaped by the forces that surround you. The facts that Christ died and rose for you, forgives you, and deserves total obedience to His commands aren't ideas you can redefine or redesign. They aren't open for negotiation. You don't swap them to win points with people.

Sometimes you can act, talk, dress, and think in a way that is seen as wonderful by both God and the people around you (2 Corinthians 8:21, Hebrews 12:14). Other times you can't. It's a choice. But it's no contest whose opinion matters more (Luke 12:4–5).

Am I now trying to win the approval of men, or of God? Or am I trying to please men? If I were still trying to please men, I would not be a servant of Christ.

GALATIANS 1:10

21

Cable Surfing All Alone

There wasn't even anything on TV. Sixty-two cable stations and Nina's best choices were a demo of the lesser-known features of spreadsheet software, a shopping network hawking ceramic kittens, and a local-access rerun of a third-grade boys' basketball game. Too much fun.

Nina agreed with her parents that her school's dances weren't the best place to be. She'd been there. She'd seen what went on. So she didn't go. Normally she didn't feel left out because she always found something to do with her family or friends. This time, though, her friends weren't around, her dad was away on business, and her mom was busy with Nina's sick little brother.

So at seven o'clock that evening when the dance was starting, Nina curled up on her bed and stared at the wall, imagining the fun she was missing.

📭 **Read Psalm 1:1–6. What does God promise you when you feel like a reject because of Him?**

You feel like a tree stuck by your lonesome on the prairie, bent by the wind, scraggly for lack of water. No one ever lops a gushing hose at your roots. No one ever trims you to look like a giraffe or a flamingo. You fear you're going to lose your leaves, shrivel up, then tumble away in the wind.

You may have convinced yourself that's what you are. Or you might worry that's what you'll become if you refuse to wallow with the wicked or saddle up with sinners or mesh with those who mock God. All the fun you'll miss roars in your imagination.

It's time to remember reality. You're not the one who needs to worry about wilting. Here's what God promises His people: They drink from God's streams. They sprout fruit. They stand in God's presence. God watches over every detail of their lives. And here's what happens to those who distance themselves from God: They lack roots—no water, no food, no life. They're dried-out "chaff" (the husks left over from threshing wheat). They're blown away in the hurricane of God's judgment.

It doesn't sound like you're missing much.

Blessed is the man who does not walk in the counsel of the wicked or stand in the way of sinners or sit in the seat of mockers.

PSALM 1:1

22

A Sea of Eyeballs

Tony thought Lindsey was fascinating—even in an ugly phys ed outfit.

Lindsey was, well, mature. The other guys made smutty comments about her, but Tony just contemplated how cool it would be if she was his girlfriend. He would be famous, or something like that, and more.

"You know you're dreaming about her," they yelled at Tony as he stood watching her. Dazed by Lindsey, he didn't hear. "Forget it, Tony. She thinks you're a moron." Still he didn't break his stare.

So the guys winged Tony the basketball to wake him up. The ball, however, didn't slam his chest or knock the wind from his gut. It smashed into his face, shattering his glasses and busting his nose.

Tony was in for a difficult time explaining to his mother why he missed the pass.

▶ **Read Matthew 5:27–30. How does Jesus want you to relate to the opposite sex?**

If guys or girls gouged an eye every time their thoughts got hot, the ground would be littered with eyeballs. Everywhere you look and listen—magazines, TV, movies, software, jokes, videos, T-shirts, billboards—you're encouraged to let your thoughts wander to sex.

What Jesus calls "lust" isn't mere curiousity about the opposite sex. It isn't wanting a really close friend—or even, as you get older, having a body that feels sexually hungry. Lust is grasping for *what* you can't have *when* you can't have it.

The Bible is clear that "adultery," sex outside of marriage, is wrong (Exodus 20:14, Hebrews 13:4). But Jesus says purity runs deeper than that. You don't have to roam under clothes or get pregnant to have gone "too far." Real purity is booting from your brain even thoughts of wrong things.

That's what Jesus means by His hyped-up language ("hyperbole") about getting rid of things that cause you to sin. Jesus doesn't want you to mutilate yourself, but to cut off evil—to exit situations that tempt you, look the other way when you need to (Job 31:1), and crowd out bad thoughts by filling your head with good ones.

Like someone has said, "Even a blind man can lust." Plucking out an eye isn't purity.

But I tell you that anyone who looks at a woman lustfully has already committed adultery with her in his heart.

MATTHEW 5:28

58

23

Awash in a Pool of Drool

"The inverse of the common denominator is multiplied by the square root of the algebraic cosine," your teacher drones, "which of course demonstrates that if x is greater than or equal to y, then z is the negative product of an imaginary number."

The rest is a haze. Mr. Ultradull keeps lecturing, too slow to see you're losing consciousness in the back of his room. As you drift off to sleepy-bye you wonder if there are laws against a teacher being so boring.

Half an hour later the bell rings.

You awake. Your face rests on your desk in a pool of drool.

Through sleepy eyes you see the last of your classmates exiting the room. You stumble after them and wipe your face on your sleeves, only to notice that the front of your shirt has sopped up spit like a sponge. You're soaked.

You wish you could wake up. Only you're not dreaming.

▶ **Read Galatians 5:13–15. Do all friends leave teeth marks?**

You sass each other. You tell each other's secrets and talk behind each other's backs. You're into borrowing without asking (aka stealing) from each other. You tease, but bury in the teases stinging bits of truth. You get in ugly moods and won't say why. Even the best of friendships often flip-flop between kindness and cutdowns, fondness and fights, cool times and cruelty.

They bite you. You bite back. That's life with friends. Isn't it?

Or is it?

Right before the passage you read, Paul had finished saying that the big deal about being a Christian isn't rules and rituals. It's that God loves us. So we love one another.

No one normal wants to go through life alone. But you know that just any old friend won't do. You need friends who keep you from making a fool of yourself. Friends who keep you from destroying yourself. Friends who wake you up before you drool on the desk. And friends who stick with you even when your shirt is soaked.

But that only happens when you search for friends who count. And call a truce.

The entire law is summed up in a single command: "Love your neighbor as yourself." If you keep on biting and devouring each other, watch out or you will be destroyed by each other.

GALATIANS 5:14–15

part 3

hangin' tight

24

Why Doesn't He Blow My Locker Open?

Your parents told you being a Christian was "the most important thing in life."

No one else seemed to think so.

Your youth pastor said you were supposed to "live for God" at school and "take a stand." God would be with you.

So where was He? *If God loves me*, you've been wondering, *why doesn't He blow my locker open?* You know—with some mind-melting display of power. You twiddle the lock and suddenly KABOOM, your locker door hangs by half a hinge. When the dust clears, you see God's blinding shining face talking to you, giving you a message for your school. Light fills the hall and your classmates fall to their knees in awe of God and respect for you, God's spokesperson in their midst.

It would be most impressive.

Read 1 Kings 19:9–18. This passage picks up in the middle of the story of the Old Testament prophet Elijah, who has just fled into the desert to avoid being killed by a thoroughly nasty queen. What did God do for Elijah when he felt like giving up?

Only a month had passed since Elijah stood on Mt. Carmel, one man against 450 prophets of the fake god Baal. At Elijah's request, God flung fire from heaven to torch a sacrifice—stone altar and all. Baal failed. God won. Elijah was a hit, for a while.

What did Elijah get for doing everything right? He stood alone, or so he thought. Everyone else in Israel, he said, had abandoned their faith in the one true God to follow idols. And Queen Jezebel wanted to kill him. Elijah told God, "I have had enough!" (19:4). Lonely and scared, he wanted to lie down and die.

When Elijah despaired, God showed him afresh who He was—not in an earthquake, wind, or fire, but in a whisper. God gave him a partner—Elisha. And God told him he wasn't really alone. *Elijah had friends*—7,000 other worshipers of God.

By raising Christ from the dead, God has already done an untoppable, unstoppable awesome-display-of-power thing for you. Now He wants to give you partners, to open your eyes to see the other believers on your side.

But you have to be able to spot 'em before you can join 'em.

———————

He replied, "I have been very zealous for the LORD God Almighty. The Israelites have rejected your covenant, broken down your altars, and put your prophets to death with the sword. I am the only one left, and now they are trying to kill me too."

1 KINGS 19:10

25

A Band Called Waffle Vomit

The lead singer of the band Waffle Vomit stared down from posters all over Kurt's bedroom. "He has songs about prayer and stuff," Kurt told his older brother Jeff. "He's got to be a Christian."

Jeff rolled his eyes. "Sure, Kurt. He's foaming at the mouth because he's a rabid follower of Jesus. That's why he looks like he chews eyeballs for breakfast."

"That's just a ploy," Kurt explained. "No one would listen to him if he didn't dress like that. Besides—we're not supposed to judge."

"We're not supposed to condemn people and throw away the key," Jeff corrected. "But don't you think we're supposed to be able to tell who's a Christian?"

📖 **Read Ephesians 2:1–5. How do you know who is a Christian and who isn't?**

If a dead man were propped up in an easy chair with a newspaper and slippers, it might be hard to judge from across the room whether he was dead or just relaxing. But the closer you got the more you would know—a whiff or a poke tells you a lot. Other times it takes a pulse check or a search for brain waves. And there are a few cases—usually victims of tragic accidents—where only God can distinguish life from death.

It doesn't usually take the county coroner to tell a dead body from a live one.

You don't have to be a pastor to know a Christian when you see one. Being a Christian isn't going to church or being nice or talking religious. It's having God's new life.

Without God, the part of you that wants to be friends with God is dead. Even if you look good, propped up on the outside, your insides are dead in disobedience—you've done what *you* want, not what God wants. But when you become a Christian, God freely forgives you. He makes you His friend and jump starts your heart. Once you were dead toward God. Now you're "alive with Christ." You start to follow the One who saved you.

Sometimes when a person is reborn (John 3:1–16) you don't see much life right away—you can't see the new friendship with God that's formed on the inside. But God's life doesn't take long to ooze to the outside to affect attitudes and actions.

You spot a Christian by the new life that's begun. Life grows. Life shows.

But because of his great love for us, God, who is rich in mercy, made us alive with Christ even when we were dead in transgressions—it is by grace you have been saved.

EPHESIANS 2:4–5

26

Head Above Water

"I guess I never thought of that, Mrs. Dalbey," Halley mumbled.

Christy gave her mom a look that said "Tell her more!" So she did.

"There's a reason God sometimes doesn't seem real to us, Halley," Mrs. Dalbey said quietly. "The things each of us has done wrong are a lot worse than we think. They're sins that separate us from God. They make us His enemies."

Halley listened closely as Mrs. Dalbey continued. "God says we deserve death—eternal separation from Him—for our sins. Except that God's Son—Jesus— took that punishment when He died on the cross. If we admit our sin and accept the fact that Jesus died for us, God forgives us. That's how each of us be- comes a Christian. When you get to know Jesus and act on what you believe, it starts to feel real."

Mrs. Dalbey let Halley chew on that for a while. Then she asked if Halley wanted to pray to start a new relationship with God. She did. "God, I know I need you," they prayed together. "I've sinned. Thank you that Jesus died in my place for my sins. I want your forgiveness. I want to follow and obey you."

✔ Read Colossians 1:9–14. What does it mean for God to "rescue" us?

Christians aren't corpses. They're alive. But what does that look like? People, after all, can look alive but not be energized by God's new life. They're propped up and well preserved, but they haven't come to know God. They're still dead on the inside.

So what's the first sign of God's life? You know you're *rescued* by God.

If you're in water over your head and don't know how to swim, you can pretend for only so long that you don't need help. The beginning point in becoming a Christian is realizing that you're in water way past your eyeballs. The bad stuff you've done and the good stuff you've left undone has plunged you deep in sin. If you say you never sin, you're lying to yourself (1 John 1:8). And the penalty for sin is separation from God forever (Romans 6:23).

But God doesn't leave you to rescue yourself, to yank yourself to safety by your swimsuit. If you admit your sin to God, He forgives you (1 John 1:9). He saves you from your life-or-death problem of sin. He rescues you from drowning.

For he has rescued us from the dominion of darkness
and brought us into the kingdom of the Son he loves,
in whom we have redemption,
the forgiveness of sins.

COLOSSIANS 1:13–14

27

It's Not a Small World After All

"That was truly wonderful," you say to your hosts. "I want to do it again."

With that, your tiny boat glides off on another spine-tingling tour. Multicultural munchkins brighten your day as they sing "It's A Small World After All" over and over—and over—in 687 different languages.

After your fourteenth trip, your hosts are exasperated. "May we suggest that you look at your map?" they urge. "Really. There are many other attractions in the park."

"This *is* the park," you protest. You slap at the map they offer and instead pull out some papers and wave them in front of the attendants. "This is it. The deed to DisneyWorld. *And* Epcot Center. My father gave it to me, and here I am. Enjoying it fully, I might add. Another round please."

"Whatever you say," they reply, unwilling to force you to go where you don't want to go.

▶ Read Titus 2:11–14. What does it mean for you to be "remade" by God?

If you owned DisneyWorld and Epcot Center you wouldn't be content to float your boat and listen to motorized mannequins in *la-la* land. Within minutes you would be off on another ride. Within days you would know the location of every attraction in the parks. And years later you would know every inch of your territory. But if you didn't look at your map and go exploring you might never know that more existed.

Being immature as a Christian is like staying stuck on the first ride you find. Sometimes those of us who are Christians—those who have let God rescue them—don't realize that God has more for us. A Christian is someone who is being *remade* by God.

Being a Christian—possessing "salvation"—is a lot bigger than having your sins forgiven. The word behind "to save" means "to be made whole." God doesn't just want to rescue you from drowning, but to fix the injuries you suffered and teach you how to swim. He wants to train you to say "NO!" to evil and "YES!" to good. He wants you to live closer and closer to Him. He wants you to use the Bible as a map to teach, instruct, encourage, and correct you, prying open your eyes to all that He has for you (2 Timothy 3:16–17).

Unless, of course, you choose to stay on the kiddy rides.

For the grace of God that brings salvation has appeared to all men. It teaches us to say "No" to ungodliness and worldly passions, and to live self-controlled, upright and godly lives. . . .

Titus 2:11–12

28

Turn on a Dime

As Bryan swept the garage he felt sick to his stomach.

Last night Bryan and his brother Trent were having a quick snack before bed. Trent wouldn't stop teasing Bryan, and Bryan got so mad that he hurled a plate across the kitchen at his brother. He missed, but it gouged the cupboard and shattered on the floor. *What was I thinking?* Bryan was a Christian. He couldn't understand why he still got angry at his brother.

By the time Bryan finished mowing the lawn he felt even worse. He just couldn't shake what he had seen on his mom's face after the fight with Trent. She wasn't a Christian. And she looked at him like he was a mass murderer. She might as well have said it: "You phony! I thought Christians were supposed to be different."

What do I do now?

☑ **Read 1 John 1:9–2:6. How can a Christian stay close to God?**

It doesn't take long to notice that Christians aren't perfect. That's even clear in the Bible. John writes that if we know God we obey Him. A few verses earlier he argues, though, that we're kidding ourselves if we claim to be perfect. He also says he writes so that we won't sin, yet points out that Jesus' death (His "atoning sacrifice") means that forgiveness is available to any believer who needs it.

Here's the scoop: As a Christian you're *rescued* from sin and hell. But you're not fully *remade*. In the meantime you need to be *responsive*.

A car that's responsive takes barely a twitch on the steering wheel to turn it. An old car with sloppy handling will hardly budge no matter how hard you crank the wheel. To John, a responsive Christian is one who admits his or her sin and asks forgiveness. Paul said it almost the same: A responsive Christian is one who gets up and goes on after falling down (Philippians 3:12–14).

That's *your* goal. And it's the best kind of friend you could ever find. If you want friends who really count, start by looking for the *rescued*—the ones who know God. Then look for those who are being *remade*—the ones who are growing. And if you find a friend who's *responsive* to God—one who turns when God says, "Turn!"—hang on tight.

My dear children, I write this to you so that you will not sin. But if anybody does sin, we have one who speaks to the Father in our defense—Jesus Christ, the Righteous One. He is the atoning sacrifice for our sins, and not only for ours but also for the sins of the whole world.

1 JOHN 2:1–2

29

More Than Skin Deep

Jennifer quizzed Jason. "You're wearing your shirt tomorrow, aren't you?" Their youth group had all bought T-shirts with the group's logo. Jason had bought one too, but he felt stupid wearing it to church, much less anywhere else. As far as shirts went it was cool, except people always asked him questions he couldn't answer. But it would look bad if he didn't wear his shirt the next day. He was supposed to help advertise a concert that week.

"It's dirty," Jason lied.

"Won't your mom wash it?"

"I do my own laundry," he lied again. "I won't have time tonight."

"Don't be a dirtball. We're all wearing them. How else will people know about the concert?"

Jason was worn out. "Okay, okay. I'll wear it." He showed up the next day with it hidden under a big flannel shirt. Jennifer saw him. She told him that didn't count.

▶ **Read Acts 2:42–47, which describes the very first Christians. What good are Christian friends?**

Strange things pull friends together. *Good things*: sports, hobbies, after-school clubs. *Hard things*: alcoholic parents, busted-up families, tough home-work. *Stupid things*: potty mouths, slamming people, inhaling, drinking, huge houses.

But at least *something* pulls you together. You have things in common.

God doesn't plan for friendships between Christians to be like a bad party where you sit and stare at each other because you can't think of anything to talk about. And He wants your bond with other Christians to grow beyond wearing matching T-shirts.

Your job isn't to stick out, but to stick together.

The passage you read and the rest of the book of Acts details how the early church hung close. They clung to each other without becoming a clique. They took care of one another. They shared their stuff. They went around doing good. They got close to Christ. They told the world about Jesus. They were an always-expanding family.

They stood out for more than their shirts (John 13:35).

———————

Every day they continued to meet together in the temple courts. They broke bread in their homes and ate together with glad and sincere hearts, praising God and enjoying the favor of all the people. And the Lord added to their number daily those who were being saved.

ACTS 2:46–47

74

30

Pray for One Another

"What's wrong?" Matt poked Aimee in the side, trying to get her to smile.

"Nothing," Aimee mumbled.

Danay didn't believe her. "Then why are you sitting here all by yourself?"

That made Aimee crumple into a cry. "My dad told us last night that he and mom are getting a divorce."

"No way!" Matt laughed. "Your parents are great. You're not serious. Are you?"

Danay hit Matt. "She's serious, Matt. Stop it."

Aimee told Danay and Matt about how her parents acted so nice whenever people were around, but walloped each other as soon as they were alone. Matt apologized for laughing, and after a while he said they should pray for Aimee. Right there. Right then. So Matt and Danay prayed very simply that God would take care of Aimee and do whatever He could to help her parents.

☑ **Read Ephesians 6:18. How can you pray for friends?**

You probably don't dissect your conversations with friends the way you slice and study a frog in biology class. You just talk. Prayer, though, might not be so easy. But in this one verse Paul dissects prayer to show how prayer—talking to God—is put together:

"Pray in the Spirit" is the hardest part to understand, but it says *how* to pray: Ask God to spark your prayers and to help you want what He wants.

"On all occasions" says *where* to pray: Prayer works when you're alone, but becomes even more powerful when you pray with other Christians (Matthew 18:19–20). And hey—talking to God along with them isn't meant to be any more complicated than talking to one friend in front of another friend. Keep it simple. No frothy words.

"All kinds of prayers and requests" tells you *what* to pray about: Everything!

"Always keep on praying" describes *when* to pray: As often as you breathe.

"All the saints" says *who* to pray for: Start with your Christian friends.

One question left. *Why* pray? Paul doesn't say, because it's an assumption behind everything else he wrote. You pray because you and the people you know need God. Because they need His help. And because God wants to answer (1 John 5:14–15).

And pray in the Spirit on all occasions with all kinds of prayers and requests. With this in mind, be alert and always keep on praying for all the saints.

EPHESIANS 6:18

31
Talk It Up

Janelle did the "secret angel" thing the whole retreat. She wrapped a small present and snuck it into the cabin of the girl whose name she had drawn. She wrote a page-long note detailing everything she liked about her "mortal." She slyly volunteered to clean up the breakfast dishes when it was actually her mortal's turn.

She had no idea who had her own name. She hoped it wasn't the girl who barfed on her in the dining hall. It probably wasn't the guy who decked her on the skating rink.

On the last night of the retreat everyone flopped on their stomachs in a circle, a single candle in the middle lighting the room. One by one, each person told who he or she had drawn and said something profound: "I like your shirt. Can I have it?" "I don't know who you are, but you're really nice." Janelle described how she saw her mortal being kind to someone. Everyone clapped for her mortal.

No one said anything about Janelle. They had lost her name.

Read Hebrews 3:12–13. How can you encourage your Christian friends?

Encouraging each other isn't group hugs. It isn't forcing gooshy feelings the way you wring the last

bubble of toothpaste from a tube. It's inspiring someone's confidence—their courage. It's helping a friend
climb higher.

The writer of Hebrews warned that it's possible for
any of us to be duped into thinking sin looks good
and God looks bad. The remedy? Daily doses of reality dropped kindly on us by other Christians.

Encouragement means reminding a friend *who
God is*: God never makes dumb rules (Psalm 19:7–9).
He's good and loving in everything He does (Psalm
145:17). Encouragement means reminding a friend
what's right: obeying parents (Colossians 3:20), gulp-
ing back gossip (James 1:26), speaking with purity
about the opposite sex (Ephesians 5:3–4), plus lots of
other things you know are right. And encouragement
means reminding a friend that *you'll make it together*
(2 Timothy 2:22).

You don't have to say much. But you need to talk
it up. If you and your friends don't encourage each
other, who will?

---

*But encourage one another daily, as long as it is
called Today, so that none of you may be hardened
by sin's deceitfulness.*

HEBREWS 3:13

78

32

It's a Team Thang

"She needs an answer *now!*" Clayton whined, muffling the phone against his shirt.

"We've talked about this before," Clayton's mom answered calmly. "We don't think it's appropriate for you to go out with Julie alone."

"We're not going out. We're just going to the mall. Don't you trust me?"

"It's not a question of trust, Clayton. It's not wise to put yourself in a situation where—"

"The kids at church are going to a hockey game tonight," Clayton's dad broke in. "You said you might go to that. Why don't you invite Julie to go with you? We'll even pay. You can treat her."

Problem solved, Mom and Dad supposed. Clayton thought not. "I don't want to bring Julie around the kids at church. She'll think I'm one of them."

Read Proverbs 16:18. What happens when you think you can survive alone as a Christian?

You may not be tempted to watch toxic rental videos or listen to nasty run-dogs-over-with-tanks music or sneak into a casino to blackjack away your college savings. But at times you may dream of ditching your Christian friends for bigger and better things.

You might laugh if people—like your parents—think you're tottering on the fence between obedience and disobedience, between living as a Christian and wandering away from God. But most people who stop being Christians don't dash toward the fence and pole vault over to the other side. They try to tiptoe along the top of the fence.

That's when they need other believers to call them back from the edge—when, for example, they want to go with non-Christians, or they decide they'll do *anything* to be popular, or they choose to make minor stuff like clothes or money majorly important.

If you ignore the pleas of your friends and do a dance on the fence, sooner or later you'll slip. Don't be surprised if it hurts to body slam into the ground on the other side. There's no one over there waiting to catch you.

———————

Pride goes before destruction,
a haughty spirit before a fall.

PROVERBS 16:18

33

It's Your Decision, Dear

Samantha felt a little uncomfortable wearing a long skirt to her first debate. Sam never wore "girl clothes." But it felt good to dress up. She had been picked to fire the first shots in a debate about how to protect endangered species. Sam's side would argue that the government couldn't use environmental regulations to seize private property.

Sam had tried running cross-country. She was slow. She made cheerleading, but they just trailed boys they thought were cute and teased girls who didn't make the squad. Sam didn't think there were any other Christians on the debate team, but the advisors and other students were fun. She got to stretch her brain. Finally she fit.

Once after shredding another team and sending them home crying, Sam was asked to join a weekend tournament team. Great—until Sam realized she wouldn't have time for church for a few months. Sam's mom said she had to make her own decision.

Suddenly it was Sam who felt like crying.

Read 1 Corinthians 10:13. How do you do what's right when you're all alone?

You don't live in a bubble. Your world, you might have noticed, isn't very Christian. Your Christian

81

friends aren't always around. You aren't even fitted with a pressurized space suit to keep you from exploding when you venture out alone into spiritual nothingness.

Like every other Christian, you'll face temptations to do wrong. (It's "common to man.") But it doesn't always come in scary offers of sex and drugs. The biggest temptation you'll face is this: To stop paying attention to God. To do well without Him. To ease Him out of your life. To be like the fool who says, "There is no God" (Psalm 14:1). The fool doesn't mean that God doesn't exist. He means that God doesn't matter.

Often it's you, God, and a temptation—no one looking, no Christian friends to pull you back. In those moments, the decision to obey God—to make Him matter—is yours alone.

God always provides a way to choose for Him. You may not see it at first. But choosing to hunt for His way out is the first step in choosing to make Him matter.

No temptation has seized you except what is common to man. And God is faithful; he will not let you be tempted beyond what you can bear. But when you are tempted, he will also provide a way out so that you can stand up under it.

1 CORINTHAINS 10:13

34

High Voltage

"I sure don't have anything to say," Maria sighed. "My parents are Christians. My grandparents are Christians. I grew up a Christian. I'm a boring—"

Maria's youth pastor, Michelle, stuck her head in the door. "How's it coming?" she asked. Michelle had stuck Maria and five other kids in a room to make them brainstorm how to tell other students at school about Christ. An experiment, she said.

"We could have a visitor's night at church. We could have games, skits, and free pizza," Shelly bubbled. "We might even—"

Scott interrupted. "Nick thought we should have a Bible study before school," he jeered. "You couldn't even get *us* to come to that." Nick turned red.

Michelle glared at Scott. "Actually, both of those are good starts. Okay. Here's the next step. Both of those tactics mean that your non-Christians friends have to come to *you*. You're with those people all day long. How could you use that time?"

That got them thinking.

> **Read 1 Peter 2:9–10. What qualifies you to tell others about Christ?**

Picture you and your Christian friends. You've started hanging together. Praying for one another.

Encouraging each other with kind words and actions—or at least working at all of that. You're charged.

You'll short-circuit and blow a fuse if all that energy stays in one place.

When God formed the church, the first believers grew up. They also grew out. Jesus told His followers to "go and make disciples" (Matthew 28:18). They did. God "added to their number daily those who were being saved" (Acts 2:47). They told the world about Christ and His love—always with actions, often with words. Instead of becoming a clique, they became a family. Instead of turning inward, they spread out.

You might think you have nothing to tell. You probably didn't rack up a bunch of gory, sensational sins for God to save you from. Your decision to follow Christ may have been quiet, made over time. But if you understand God's "mercy"—how God forgave, accepted, and befriended you—then you have a story. You belong to God. Tell people about the God who called you to live close to himself.

But you are a chosen people, a royal priesthood, a holy nation, a people belonging to God, that you may declare the praises of him who called you out of darkness into his wonderful light. Once you were not a people, but now you are the people of God; once you had not received mercy, but now you have received mercy.

1 PETER 2:9–10

part 4

stickin' close

35

All You Have and All You Need

With two intense Christian friends always close by, Jon had it made. Jon, Josh, and Tim went to the same church, the same school, even lived on the same block.

But then Josh moved away. A few months later, Tim started making excuses for not showing up at church. Then he started dodging Jon altogether. When Jon called to go blading, Tim's older sister lied that he wasn't home. The last time they sort of talked, Tim answered the phone himself. When he recognized Jon on the other end—*click.*

Jon heard that Tim's dad had started telling him it was stupid to be a Christian. After a while Tim thought it was stupid too.

So Jon was stuck by himself.

He knew it wasn't supposed to be that way.

But that's how it was.

> **Read Psalm 142:1–7. What do you do when you feel alone?**

It feels like you're lost a long way from home. You're alone—the only Christian your age you can spot. Or—pretty likely—your Christian friends attend other schools or at least have other teachers. Or maybe the Christian friends you did find have stopped being kind.

Sooner or later your Christian friends let you down. Sooner or later there's no one around. Christian friendships are supposed to be a shelter, and usually they are. But once in a while you get left out in the rain. That's the time to find your way to God.

God sometimes allows you to feel alone so you learn to hide in Him.

The top of Psalm 142 says that David wrote the psalm in a cave, possibly when Israel's King Saul had gone insane and wanted to kill him (1 Samuel 22:1–2).

So what did David do in the cave? He hid from his enemies. He prayed. He learned to trust. He got to know the God who says over and over "I will never leave you or forsake you" (Joshua 1:5; Hebrews 13:5). He got to know the God who sticks close when no one else does. And an odd thing happened. When David hid in the cave—in God—his family came and supported him. So did a bunch of friends.

I cry to you, O Lord; I say, "You are my refuge. . . ."

PSALM 142:5

36

Saved From Sludgedom

"Swank, huh?" Papa Sludge says to his family as they spy the mansion high on a hill, lit up in the moonlight. "Toldja it'd be great." Pops maneuvers the family truckster past the front gate, running over the valet who offers to park the car. Pops jams their rusted purple Lincoln into a tiny spot on the lawn, and out piles Pops, Mama, and fourteen little ones, dinging doors on both sides.

The greasy horde follows the hundreds of candles lighting the way up the driveway to the house, bursting into a ballroom of long-gowned ladies and tuxedoed gentlemen. Grabbing fistfuls of elegant appetizers, they flop on a couch in front of a TV the size of one of those walls at a mall. As they claw for the remote control, it drops and shatters, with the tube locked on *WWF Wrestling*.

"Poyfect," Pops exclaims. He kicks his shoes off onto a glass coffee table. "Hey yous," he yells to the host. "Hows about a foot rub?"

📖 **Read Psalm 15:1–5. What does God expect of you if you want to live close to Him?**

Pick a part at the party. As a Christian you are (a) the valet who gets run over (b) one of the well-washed, well-heeled partygoers or (c) a member of the family Sludge.

The right pick is *c*. We're all grungy before we get to know God.

But also *b*. We don't stay that way.

Getting to know God isn't like showing up at a party hideously underdressed, an object of sneers. Because each of us sins, none of us is good enough to approach God on our own—to live on God's "holy hill." Yet God loved us while we were filthy with sin (Romans 5:8). And God makes us good enough to be in His totally pure presence, making us right with himself through Christ's death, flinging open the gates and inviting us in (Hebrews 10:19–23). God and His partygoers welcome the unwelcomable.

Yet it isn't right to stay sludgy, to spew on God's kindness. We're no longer unaware of our mess of sin. So we learn to stop running over people and insulting our Host. It's fitting that those who live on the hill act like the one who owns the house.

If we keep on being rude and crude we won't enjoy the party.

———————

Lord, who may dwell in your sanctuary? Who may live on your holy hill? He whose walk is blameless and who does what is righteous, who speaks the truth from his heart.

Psalm 15:1–2

37

All Ears

"Not now!" Jill's dad barked. "I'm worn out and I have work to do!"

"But I need help with math," Jill repeated. "It's due tomorrow."

"You're going to have to figure it out yourself," Mr. Davidson came back. "Maybe if you and your sister didn't fight all the time I'd have energy to help you."

Jill's mom rushed to calm dad down. "What do you think it's like for your father? He works all day long and comes home and hears you screaming at each other."

By then Jill's little sister was pulling at Mr. Davidson's pant leg. "Will you take me to the park?" Mr. Davidson flashed a tiny bit of tenderness, then flew off again.

"I have to work," he said, pulling his coat on. "I'm going back down to the office. Good-night." Jill winced when the door slammed behind him. She wondered why she even tried to talk to her dad.

☛ **Read Psalm 27:7–14. Why does God sometimes seem hard of hearing?**

Talking to a parent can be like talking to a rock. A big, silent, unbudgeable rock. Or a sharp stone flung hard at your head. Or an annoying little rock in your shoe. Some kids react by shutting up and only talking with their friends. You're fortunate if you can talk back and forth well with your parents—you probably know friends who can't.

God isn't like a parent who can't hear or won't talk.

Still, sometimes He seems far off. Even David begged God to hear him and respond. What David wrote in Psalm 27, though, hints at some reasons God goes quiet: To teach you to seek Him more, to not treat Him like an old toy you store on the shelf until you're in the mood. To teach you to trust His acceptance of you, that if you admit your sin to Him, He never holds it against you (Psalm 103:12). And to test whether you want to know how to follow Him badly enough to wait for Him to show you.

In the end God wants to see one thing built in you: confidence that He is good and He is your God. He isn't teasing. He isn't too busy. He's teaching.

It may feel like you're alone. You're not. Sitting in a room too dark to see anything doesn't mean God isn't there.

———

Wait for the LORD; be strong and take heart
and wait for the LORD.

PSALM 27:14

38

Zero Tolerance

Adam waited outside the school office while the principal talked to his mom. An hour earlier one of the school's counselors—the one in charge of discipline—had yanked him from class. As they stood in the hallway, the counselor and another teacher said someone saw a knife in Adam's backpack. They wanted to turn Adam's pack inside out.

They said he had it. Adam said he didn't. They opened up his backpack and there it was, a small pocketknife. It wasn't Adam's. He didn't put it there.

Adam went pale and started to explain, but he knew they wouldn't believe him. "Zero Tolerance" meant they didn't care who the knife belonged to or how it got there. They wouldn't even try to find out. It was in Adam's backpack, and he was automatically out for the rest of the school year, a three-month suspension. Lots of time to stew.

✔ **Read Psalm 26:1–12. Does anyone know you're right when everyone says you're wrong?**

You've *fwopped* your little brother on the head plenty of times and didn't get caught. For once you were actually being nice, but that's not what your parents think. They ground you.

Your protests of innocence sound hollow. Get over it.

But there's another kind of false accusation that's harder to swallow. You walk into a clothing store. One glance from the manager and your age makes you an instant shoplifting suspect. You laugh at a story you overhear after school at practice. Then you figure out everyone's talking about you—and it's not true. Or you choose to hang out with one friend. Suddenly another friend thinks you're evil.

To be "blameless" in the Bible goes beyond being able to say you didn't do wrong—*this* time. It's being absolutely sure that your one goal has been to do God's will, to obey in the power of His truth and love. You didn't join those plotting to do wrong. You did your best to do right.

David was sure of his innocence. No one believed him, he claimed.

God did. He knows the truth. And He promises that one day everyone else will know too (1 Corinthians 3:12–13).

Vindicate me, O Lord, for I have led a blameless life;
I have trusted in the Lord without wavering.

Psalm 26:1

39

You Can't Run and You Can't Hide

David woke at the noise of the VCR swallowing a tape and the TV flicking on. "What are you doing?" he asked, tangled in his sleeping bag. "What time is it?"

"Shhh," Cal hushed. "I brought some midnight entertainment."

By now the four other guys sleeping in David's basement were awake too.

"What is it?" Billy begged. "Tell me it's the swimsuit edition tape—pleeease?"

"This is no swimsuit video. This is better," Cal promised.

For a second David saw the bodies onscreen. "My parents—!" was all his shocked brain could blurt out.

"Trust me," Cal said as he sat back to watch. "Don't they sleep?"

"Not tonight," boomed David's dad from the bottom of the steps as he flipped on the lights.

☑ **Read Psalm 32:1–11. What happens when you try to hide from God?**

You've probably felt that sickening snarl in your stomach followed by the need to crawl in a corner and rot. You're embarrassed because you did something idiotic—or even ashamed because you did

95

something wrong (what this psalm calls "sins" and "transgressions" and "iniquity"). You want no one to know. Not your friends, not your parents, not even God.

You can't live like that.

Sometimes you feel guilty for nothing—like if the blame for sins you feel bad about actually belongs on someone else. But if you know you've done wrong and you haven't made it right with God, at least part of the pain you feel is from Him. It's meant to prick you, to push you to Him. You could choose to wallow in your badness or to clamp your conscience, but God would rather have you choose to let Him help you. You can't rescue yourself. You can't remake yourself. God can.

It's scary when someone can see everything about you. You can't hide. Then again, with God you don't have to—He knows you inside and out anyway. And it's good to be known for who you are. No better, no worse, just the real you.

God hates when you suffer by yourself. He wants you to hide *in* Him, not *from* Him.

———————

When I kept silent, my bones wasted away through my groaning all day long. . . . Then I acknowledged my sin to you and did not cover up my iniquity. I said, "I will confess my transgressions to the LORD*"—and you forgave the guilt of my sin.*

PSALM 32:3, 5

40

Between Disasters

Katie's long bangs mostly hid the huge scar high on her forehead. She knew that the jagged mark wasn't pretty, but it reminded her what she had survived. Two years before she had been riding next to her dad in their pickup truck down a country highway. Another driver slid through a stop sign. The pickup slammed into the corner of that car, hitting hard enough that Katie put her head through the windshield.

At first she was so drugged she hardly knew who she was. When the doctors took her off painkillers she had to fight to not scream.

Strange—Katie almost wished she could go back to that time. God seemed so close. People prayed for her and with her constantly. When she got tired of headaches and surgeries and shots, God was tough for her. She promised God if she got well that her whole life would belong to Him.

Looking back, Katie wasn't sure how well she was keeping her promise.

> Read Psalm 40:1–10. How do you stay close to God when your life goes great?

When you fly through a windshield, you can't hardly see God through the pain. You can't wait for

Him to yank you out of tough times, and you think it will get easier to obey God in every attitude and action once everything is okay. Yet when things go good you almost wonder if it takes a shattered skull to feel close to God.

You land quite naturally on God's lap when life sends you flying. It's not hard to figure out why you need Him.

Between disasters, though, it's tempting to scurry away and ignore God. But there's still lots to do when life goes great: You can thank God today for what He did yesterday. You have a break to take time to better understand His "will," how He wants you to live. You can help people who now need your help. You can encourage other believers ("the great assembly") when they struggle. You can tell others what God has done and what He keeps on doing.

With each experience God pulls you through, He puts a "new song in your mouth." But the lyrics won't always tell how He plucked you out of a slimy, gator-infested pit. So tell others about the calm times too.

He put a new song in my mouth, a hymn of praise to our God. Many will see and fear and put their trust in the LORD.

PSALM 40:3

41

Have a Good Holler

"Why don't you look where you're going?" Lori spewed. She had enough to worry about without Tadd running into her and splattering her books and papers on the floor. She stooped down to pick up her things.

"Look where I'm going?" Tadd sassed. "Why don't you go where you're looking?"

Very original, Lori thought. *And I know—I'd look better if I wore a hat on my butt and walked backwards.* With her crossed eyes wandering all over, no one knew where Lori was looking. Besides that, she walked a bit sideways, like a crab.

At home in her room that night Lori read her Bible the only way she could—a couple inches from her face. She broke down and cried. Then she did something she had never done before. She screamed it at God: "WHY DON'T YOU FIX ME?"

Shocked at what had slipped out, Lori covered her mouth.

And she waited for lightning to strike.

📝 **Read Psalm 13:1–6. Is it okay to yell at God?**

How long until you show up? David prayed at God. *Remember me? Or have you forgotten who I am and what I need?* Those are pretty harsh words from the mouth of the guy the Bible applauds as "a man after God's own heart" (1 Samuel 13:14). But David spoke his mind and lived to tell about it.

Big feelings simmer inside when you have confused thoughts or painful emotions or a hurting body. Sometimes harsh words boil over onto yourself, people around you, even God—*especially* toward God, the one with ultimate power and complete control.

There are a lot of reasons why you can hurt even though God is in control. (A few to gnaw on: God gives human beings the power of free choice, and humans, not God, cause pain. Jesus is God's plan to fix things. Heaven is God's total solution to pain.)

You don't have to hide your pain. David wasn't afraid to tell God about his hurts. They were real. But he always got around to thinking about a bigger reality—that God's love never quits. David didn't stop at speaking his mind and his heart. He spouted until he was able to praise God again.

How long, O LORD? Will you forget me forever? How long will you hide your face from me? How long must I wrestle with my thoughts and every day have sorrow in my heart? How long will my enemy triumph over me?

PSALM 13:1–2

42
Not So Fast

Judd had skipped enough grades to make it to Sandberg Middle School as a weaselly little nine-year-old. He was smarter than almost everyone else at school—including most of the teachers. He studied trigonometry with a tutor. He had won a nationwide writing contest for his science-fiction novel—a sparkling story of slime molds rampaging through the galaxy. He never got anything wrong on anything.

Everyone at school hated Judd.

Judd wished the kids in his neighborhood would be so nice. Every day after school he dashed home, scurried up into his backyard tree house, yanked up the rope ladder, and hid. Neighborhood kids stood below and threatened to pound his head in.

No one ever came to Judd's rescue. So he threw rocks at them until they went away.

📉 **Read Psalm 35:1–10. Will God ever deal with your enemies?**

It's weird. Mumble something nasty to yourself about an enemy and it's a bad attitude. Say it to someone else and it's gossip. Shout it at your enemy and it's picking a fight. Tell it to God and suddenly it's prayer.

How can you get away with that?

Because it's *prayer*. It's pouring out all the thoughts and feelings of your heart to God. It's asking *God* to do His thing. It isn't dishing out justice with your own hands—like an egghead paying back cruelty inflicted on him, or a madman stalking and murdering a doctor who does abortions. And it isn't begging God to carry out your whims. It's pleading to Him to halt evil and give evildoers the punishment they deserve.

Old Testament believers were a bit foggy about life after death, so their prayers against enemies usually scream "Crush them NOW, God. Don't miss your chance!" Yet the New Testament is clear that some of the payback for evil—God's judgment, or His "vengeance"—won't happen until the end of time (Revelation 19:11–21).

And that's okay. God gives even awful people a chance to respond to His kindness. His concern for now is more to reach them than to roast them (2 Peter 3:7–9).

Still impatient for God to toast your enemies this afternoon?

Not so fast. Think about it. Should He be so quick to punish you?

Contend, O LORD, with those who contend with me;
fight against those who fight against me.

PSALM 35:1

43

You've Seen This One

You sit alone in your dimly lit family room, bonding with the TV, deeply into the final twelve minutes of your favorite show. This week's superevildoer just fired up a gigawatt laser beam to slice your show's hero into a zillion pieces.

Your heart stops. *Thumpa Thumpa. Thump.*

Commercial.

Back to unreality. It's ugly. The laser beam sweeps back and forth like a pendulum—*zzzzzt zzzzzt*—inches from your hero's head, frying a hole through everything it touches. You sweat. Your stomach knots. Your every muscle tightens.

"BOO!" your Dad bursts in. "Scared you, didn't I? What's on? Oh—a rerun. In just a second his sidekick is going to—"

"Don't tell me!" you scream. You hate when someone tells you the end.

Don't be ridiculous. You already know.

📗 **Read Psalm 18:1–15 (and maybe read the whole thing if you're having a really bad day). How do you feel while waiting for God to save you from a tough situation?**

If you thought TV action or mystery show heroes were real you'd go insane. Producers can't kill off

103

their main character, but week after week they make you wonder. They get you nervous. Then they let you hang through commercials. Worse yet, they flash "To be continued . . ." just when the clock tells you danger will dissolve.

Suspense isn't so entertaining in real life.

You're ill—and you wonder when you'll get well. Your parents are planning to divorce—and you get weak waiting for court dates that drag on forever. Or you're waiting for a monster test, an important game, a big recital or concert or play—and you melt into a queasy goo. The instant before your frustration is relieved—the moment you don't know relief is right around the corner—can torture you into hopelessness.

And then it's over. You're okay. God came through for you.

He *always* does. Not always how you expect. Not always when you want. But in His time and in His way He always does. So stay loose. You know how your show will end.

I call to the Lord, who is worthy of praise, and I am saved from my enemies.

PSALM 18:3

44

Waiting for the Pumpkin

Theresa flashes a smile at the finish of her balance beam routine. She'd nailed it. Her scores flip up—her brain does quick math—first place!

Her coach sweeps her up in a huge hug. "Incredible!" she cries. Theresa's teammates crowd around her, proud of their star.

By the next morning back at school everyone has heard that Theresa won the state overall junior title. Her classmates look at her with awe. They chat about her chances of making it to the Olympics.

What a year. Six months ago Theresa had just moved. She was miserable. Now she could see what God had done—a new school, a new coach, and better friends than ever before. It was great!

But when she gets a letter awarding her a full scholarship to an elite summer gymnastics camp she starts to fret. This is all getting too good to be true.

☑ **Read Psalm 118:1–16. How are you supposed to react when everything goes well?**

When life goes good you might begin to feel like Cinderella—you're having a ball but you're sure your carriage will turn back into a pumpkin.

Jesus himself warned that being a Christian

would at times be tough. "In this world you will have trouble," he said (John 16:33). Paul reminded readers that suffering is part of being a Christian (Philippians 1:29). And James explained that it often takes bad times to make us strong believers (James 1:2–4).

But when things go good—big things, little things, or everything—misery isn't the right response! Don't spoil your fun by convincing yourself it's going to blow apart in the next twelve seconds. And don't spoil yourself by thinking your success is totally your own. After all, every good gift comes straight from God (James 1:17). So celebrate good times, good things, and good friends by thanking God for what He's given.

But thanking God may not jump to mind when times are fine. When thanking Him doesn't come easy, think hard about three things: Your past—that you were surrounded, swarmed, and squashed. Your present—that God's protection and help got you where you are. And your future—that God will always be your refuge.

And say thanks.

———————

Give thanks to the LORD, for he is good;
his love endures forever.

PSALM 118:1

45
Remember When

Twice a year Luke and his dad drove to the country to visit the gravesite of Luke's mom. This time Luke's new stepmom went with them. Luke wondered what his mom would think of Denise. He liked her pretty much.

"You'd be just as tall as Mom now," Luke's dad told him. "She'd still whip you at arm wrestling, though."

"But I would crush her at hoops," Luke shot back. "Her jumpshot was feeble." Luke played a mean starting forward for his school basketball team until halfway through the season he busted his leg skiing. He had milked it for a lot of sympathy, but now the cast was off. It could have been worse.

Luke and his dad talked for a long time, while his stepmom mostly listened. It helped to sit and think—to remember the past. Before Luke's mom died of cancer three years ago, she had always said that God would take care of him.

Looking back, Luke could see that He had.

▶ Read Psalm 77:1–20. What keeps your friendship with God alive?

You plop in a chair without thinking because it's never collapsed or let you down in the past. When a friend is a proven secret-keeper, you trust him or her. You're loyal to a restaurant because they've never dropped your burger on the floor or spit in your soda.

Trust. It's built on past reliability.

You trust God best when you remember what He's done for you.

Some days you'll wonder where God has gone. *Doesn't He love me anymore? Where are the friends He promised me? Did I do something to make Him mad?* When Asaph, the author of Psalm 77, worried that God had forgotten him, he took courage from one thing: remembering God's acts in the past. Asaph thought back to the historical event in which God rescued the Israelites from slavery in Egypt ("you redeemed your people, the descendants for Jacob and Joseph"). He knew it was God who blew apart the Red Sea to let Israel escape. He was certain it was God who led the people to freedom. He hadn't seen God's footprints, yet He recognized God by His kind and powerful acts.

God has acted with kindness and power for *you* too. The same God you read about in your Bible is *your* master and friend. He sent Jesus to die and rise again for you. He's energized your heart through His Holy Spirit. He's always with you, helping you conquer your circumstances. And He's remaking you to look like Him.

Remember that. And trust.

I will remember the deeds of the LORD; yes, I will remember your miracles of long ago. I will meditate on all your works and consider all your mighty deeds.

PSALM 77:11–12

Acknowledgments

Guilty thanks to school custodians everywhere, for scrubbing off the greasespots I left on the back walls of countless classrooms, destroying any evidence that I ever sat in the back row and nodded off. And thanks to all my teachers, who made school a pretty good place to be and taught me bunches.

Heartfelt thanks to the teachers and administrators of:

Woodlake Elementary School
Richfield, Minnesota
H.O. Sonnesyn Elementary School
New Hope, Minnesota
Plymouth Junior High School
Plymouth, Minnesota
Neil A. Armstrong High School
Plymouth, Minnesota
The University of Wisconsin
River Falls, Wisconsin
National Taiwan Normal University
Taipei, Taiwan ROC
Fuller Theological Seminary
Pasadena, California

Loud thanks to Barb Lilland—my imperturbable

editor, coworker, and friend—for helping me write for early teens, and to Terry Dugan, for figuring out a way to make drool a graphic element acceptable to Gary and Carol Johnson, who themselves deserve sincere thanks for making me a double part of the Bethany family.

Warm thanks to Dick, Lana, Audrey and Jack Butler for welcoming us to our new neighborhood with cookies, walks and talks, and for letting us unload our junk at your garage sale.

A *life-and-death thanks* to Kim and Mike Sells, for keeping me sane.

And *deepest thanks* to the people who always stand with me and keep me going—Roy and Lois Johnson, Tom and Pat Benson, and especially Lyn, Nate, and Karin, my three favorite people in the world.

For Christ's Honor,
Kevin Walter Johnson